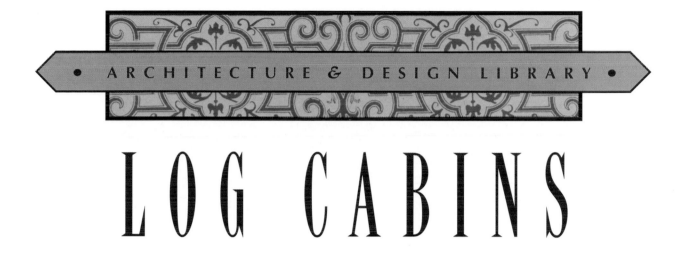

ARCHITECTURE & DESIGN LIBRARY

LOG CABINS

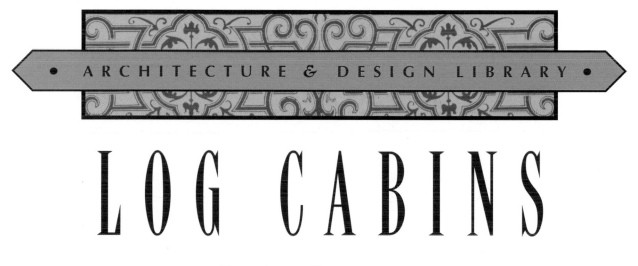

ARCHITECTURE & DESIGN LIBRARY

LOG CABINS

Janice Brewster

FRIEDMAN/FAIRFAX

PUBLISHERS

A FRIEDMAN/FAIRFAX BOOK

© 1999 by Michael Friedman Publishing Group, Inc.

Library of Congress Cataloging-in-Publication data available upon request.
ISBN 1-56799-723-6

Editor: Reka Simonsen
Art Director: Jeff Batzli
Designer: Christina Grupico
Photography Editor: Jennifer Bove
Production Director: Karen Matsu Greenberg

Color separations by Colourscan Co. Pte. Ltd.
Printed in Hong Kong by Midas Printing Limited

1 3 5 7 9 10 8 6 4 2

For bulk purchases and special sales, please contact:
Friedman/Fairfax Publishers
Attention: Sales Department
15 West 26th Street
New York, New York 10010
212/685-6610   FAX 212/685-1307

Visit our website:
http://www.metrobooks.com

To Carl, for his love and willingness to do dishes

Contents

INTRODUCTION

8

CHAPTER ONE
THE CHARM OF LOGS

18

CHAPTER TWO
THE HEART OF THE HOME

36

CHAPTER THREE
BRINGING NATURE INSIDE

48

CHAPTER FOUR
TEXTILES AND TEXTURES

68

CHAPTER FIVE
GOODS AND GEAR

82

INDEX

96

INTRODUCTION

You've seen them—some racked and abandoned, some still much loved—nestled in a grove of trees, perched by a rushing stream, standing at the edge of a stubbled cornfield, or languishing by the still waters of a lake. Log cabins call up romantic memories of idyllic settings.

Inside the cozy rooms of a log cabin, surrounded by trees that were harvested and shaped by hand, a variety of styles takes root. No matter what the particular look, each combines nostalgia for days gone by with the romance of adventure.

For centuries, pioneers, cowboys, anglers, nature lovers, and summer campers have all sought shelter in log cabins. The earliest log buildings were quite small, because they were built by hand by just one or two people. The logs had to be short enough for two men to lift and stack easily. Of course, log buildings nowadays have grown into large, sophisticated homes. Still, a simplicity of style remains at the heart of all log homes, regardless of their size.

All over the world, wherever trees grow in abundance, people in need of shelter from the elements have built homes out of logs. The construction methods vary from country to country and region to region. Every aspect of log building—from the shape of the logs to the type of corner joinery used to the way the logs are chinked—adds a layer to a cabin's style, setting it apart from other types of log cabins in other countries.

Logs make a wonderful backdrop for many different interior decorating schemes. While there's no need to slavishly follow historical precedent, logs always softly speak of their heritage. Whether you choose Western cowboy style, the refined rustic of the Adirondack tradition, the classic lines of Colonial decor, or the clean lines of Scandinavian style, you'll be tapping into a rich vein of tradition. The choices you make about your log home's architecture, its finishing touches, and its furnishings will all affect the ambience of your home.

Log cabin style is inherently comfortable and relaxed. The warm tones of wood walls underscore the feeling of informality. Creating a

OPPOSITE: *The twin slopes of a gambrel roof are reminiscent of old-fashioned barns. Unlike early cabins that tended to be dark, this home's upper floors are bathed in the light that is channeled through dormer windows. For all this home's modernity, classic cabin details remain: the front porch, the brick chimney, and the warmth of logs.*

unique style for your log cabin should be fun and easy, since it already has a great deal of personality—just play it up with the furnishings, architectural details, finishes, and accessories that make you feel good.

What's outside your cabin door? A sparkling lake in the north woods? A thick forest of evergreens? A sprawling ranch in cattle country? The setting of a log cabin, along with your personal preferences, may well influence its style. Your log cabin is a blank canvas that's yours to color. Now is the time to set the stage for log cabin style.

LEFT: *In the vast valleys of the West, towering mountains set the scene for settlers' farms and ranches. Logs were used to build homes and barns. An age-old rain barrel and a red corral gate add interest to this farmyard.*

OPPOSITE: *Old yet beloved, a pioneer farmhouse tells the tale of lives lived long ago. A shed-roofed addition has sprouted off the back of the main house, bordered by a kitchen garden. The wide logs were taken from the New World's abundant supply of huge, old trees. A fence of hand-split pickets outlines the home.*

BELOW: *The most distinctive architectural feature of log cabins is the corner notch. Here, round logs interlock with saddle notches. The natural taper of the trees remains—the narrow tree tips alternate with the wider diameter of the logs' butt ends. A draw knife is used to skin the bark from the logs, which leaves behind beautiful, subtle color variations on the surface of the logs.*

RIGHT: *For many,
log cabins and the
sun-drenched days of
summer go hand in
hand. Log cabins in
the woods and by
lakes big and small
have long provided
shelter for hunters
and anglers, retreat
for world-weary
vacationers, and
summer wilderness
adventures for
children.*

OPPOSITE: *While log cabins once housed pioneer farmers and loggers, today's log homes are often prized as meccas for leisurely pursuits. The broad decks of a handcrafted log home reach out to the edge of a swift stream and offer the luxury of a hot tub. Above, a balcony opens a bedroom to a bird's-eye view of the rushing water.*

RIGHT, TOP: *From rustic roots, today's log cabins have grown into homes filled with amenities. Still, the charm of a home fashioned from trees and reflected in the water of a placid lake remains untouched. Simple windows that once only let in light now make architectural statements. In today's homes, as in yesterday's cabins, windows frame views of the natural beauty of the outdoors.*

RIGHT, BOTTOM: *Following the back-to-the-land movement that swept North America in the 1970s, log home companies began offering kit log homes for customers who wanted to live the rustic lifestyle. This round log home, with its butt-and-pass-style corner notches, is accented by a single dormer, a varied roofline, and bright red paint on its shutters and trim.*

LEFT: *Slate blue milk paint outlines a simple kitchen window in a Finnish, square-log home, framing a view of the barn beyond. Wide windowsills are formed when thick logs are used for walls. The simple window is divided into just four panes in an unusual two-over-two configuration.*

ABOVE: *Seize the oppurtunity to let your home reflect its forest beginnings. Cedar posts on this side porch retain the fluted lines of their trunks. Peeled cedar twigs dance in an intricate pattern, replacing more mundane balusters on the porch railings. The logs' pickled finish lets the golden beauty of the flooring shine.*

CHAPTER ONE

THE CHARM OF LOGS

Logs are about the only thing common to all log cabins. The ways the logs are shaped, peeled, and fit together vary greatly from place to place, and each of these aspects has an effect on a cabin's style. Along with the logs, architectural details and special decorative touches convey the owner's love for a certain look.

The logs of a rustic cabin were left round and fitted together at the corners with rounded notches. This was a slapdash kind of housing: mud, newspaper, horsehair, or leaves were used to plug the gaps between logs. The cabin provided shelter for sleeping and little more.

Log houses that were meant to be more permanent, like those built by painstaking pioneers, featured logs that were hewn with an adze into squares or rectangles. These logs were also fitted together at the corners with intricate dovetail notches. With this style, so often seen in the Appalachian region of the United States, thick bands of chinking—a white or off-white mortar-type of adhesive—ran the length of the logs to keep wind and rain from creeping into the home. Inside, the flat logs created a surface that could be whitewashed to resemble plaster. New settlers lived on the rugged frontier, but they still wanted their homes to look civilized.

Scandinavians at home in the New World built their log cabins of round logs, but fit the logs to each other carefully. No chinking was necessary to keep the elements at bay because the logs themselves were carved in a crescent moon shape to fit snugly on top of each other.

Of course, log cabins' settings have always influenced their looks. Steeply pitched roofs helped cabins shed snow in northern climes. In warmer areas, recessed porches created shady places to escape from the heat of the midday sun.

Inside, the arrangement of rooms was dictated by necessity. The main room was gathered about the hearth. Lofts, with their low ceilings, made handy spots for sleeping. Today, despite the increase in numbers of rooms in log homes, the fireplace centered in the great room and the cozy intimacy of a loft both retain their popularity.

Log cabin style goes beyond logs—the details count, too. Windows with divided lights recall Colonial days, while those with diamond-shaped lights were the rage of the Great Camps of the Victorian era.

OPPOSITE: *Much of the appeal of the log cabin is the promise it holds for the time spent removed from the fast pace of life in hectic urban areas. A wide deck urges you to return from a fishing trip and sit for a spell, looking out over a beautiful vista and the trees that offered up the logs for your cabin.*

A cottage by the lake begs for casement windows that crank out to catch summer breezes, and because logs make thick walls, windowsills are wide, perfect for holding terra-cotta pots of herbs or pebbles collected on a hike through the woods.

Colonial style might call for a subtle bayberry or robin's-egg blue milk paint around the windows. Scandinavian traditions relish brighter colors—such as lemon yellow or hyacinth blue—employed both inside, surrounding the windows, and outside on a cabin's trim and shutters. Bold red and forest green are the signature colors of the Great Camps' classic Adirondack style.

Other details spring to mind when we think of cabins, especially an open log staircase that leads to a loft, its treads simply constructed of lengths of logs that have been split in half and worn smooth from constant use. Both the stairs and the loft boast railings formed of peeled twigs. These fanciful, twisted railings appear elsewhere, too, embracing a boathouse deck or defining the perimeter of a porch.

And speaking of porches, no log cabin would be complete without at least one. Dogtrot-style cabins were built by placing a recessed porch between two log pens, ensuring a shady, cool place to sit a spell on a sultry southern afternoon. At the lakeside cottage, a screened porch keeps mosquitoes at bay, while still offering a view of the sun setting on the water. In the Great Camps, porches were used for reading, relaxing, and socializing. On the ranch, the porch ran the full width of the house, bridging the outdoors and the indoors, and creating a space for resting and leaving dusty boots behind.

On the roof, a cabin sports wood shingles. And below, a stone foundation holds things up. Inside, round log beams and trusses remind us of the stout trunks and branches of the trees just outside. But flooring is really the basis for log cabin style. Wide planks sawn from centuries-old timbers are ideal, whether painted or left natural. Slate, cement, and rough *saltillo* tiles are also at home in a log house. Any flooring material that echoes the elements of nature is suitable.

Log cabin style can start right at the front door. Whether it's a solid wooden door with heavy wrought-iron hinges and latch or a plank door fastened together with wooden Z braces, a handmade front door introduces visitors to the home's rustic look.

The hardware that appears on the door can be continued throughout the cabin. Wrought-iron drawer pulls, light fixtures, and switchplate covers contrast beautifully with the warmth of logs. Hand-forged pieces lend authenticity to a cabin. Or skip the heavy metals and use what nature provides. The Adirondack style uses forked branches for door knobs and drapery rod holders. Use your imagination on your next walk through the woods and you'll soon discover treasures that can be put to use in your cabin.

In the kitchen and bath, cabinetry should suit the cabin's personality. Knotty pine cabinets have a cottage feel. Shelves, either left open or draped with yards of gathered calico, make an informal statement in the kitchen. At the cottage, try painting cabinets a sunny yellow or forest green. Countertops can be wood, laminate, or tile. A converted dry sink or painted dresser might make the perfect vanity for your log cabin bath. Cabinetry faced with birch bark or layered with split twigs is the epitome of high-style rustic.

And we can't forget the design impact of the logs themselves. Grain pattern, knots, and fascinating burls and cat's-eyes give each log a face all its own. The character of logs is highlighted by hand carvings depicting the cabin owner's favorite saying, a beloved dog, or a flock of geese arched against the autumn sky.

OPPOSITE: *Furnishing an outdoor room can be just as much fun as furnishing your home's interior. Sunny birch chairs with their bark intact bring the comforts of home out to the deck of this milled log home. A twig table complements the pair, and a wire plant stand elevates potted flowers to eye level.*

LEFT: *Winter is the perfect time to snuggle into the warm embrace of a log cabin. A low-slung ranch in Montana's Big Sky country makes a cozy shelter in the mountains. A broad stone chimney reveals the hearth inside.*

ABOVE: *Bright white chinking contrasts with aged round logs while sealing the home to prevent air infiltration. Red shutters made from planks set on the diagonal provide a crisp accent to the dark logs as they hang from primitive hinges, rusted with years of exposure to the elements.*

ABOVE: *Metal roofing tops this log barn and its small shed porch. While the logs for the walls were hewn square and joined with dovetail corners, the porch posts are simple round logs. An aged Stars and Stripes and a vintage rain barrel add homespun charm to the rural scene.*

ABOVE: *A stark contrast to the multifaceted log homes of today, this early home features a simple gable roof, a single door, and few windows. Still, the skill of the craftsman is apparent—in the interlocking corners of the logs, the sawn-board siding in the gable ends, and the hand-split roof shingles.*

LEFT: *On the other side of a wide-plank door, stairs lead to an upper floor. Surprisingly, the many years of footsteps have not weighed too heavily on these wooden stairs. In many small cabins, stairs would have been a space-stealing luxury—a ladder was used to climb to the loft instead.*

OPPOSITE: *Lean-tos were added to many log cabins as families grew. This addition, sided with rough-sawn boards, may have housed a summer kitchen. Bright, barn-red paint whimsically contrasts with the weathered logs and their wide bands of white chinking. A narrow picket fence encloses the kitchen garden.*

OPPOSITE: *The green of the forest is echoed in the trim of this handcrafted round-log home. The large windows mirror reflections of the sky. Wide overhangs protect the logs from the elements. The bark used as decorative inserts echoes the texture of the surrounding trees and anchors the house to its site.*

ABOVE: *A bit of the Old West is made new again. A breezeway, lined with log posts and accented by diagonal knee braces, has been enclosed with glass to create a fanciful passageway into this log home. Wood floors and creamy white plaster ceilings complement the smooth patina of the aged logs.*

LEFT: *Massive logs form a rustic background for a bay window trimmed in forest green paint. Along the window's base, twig mosaic panels recall the halcyon days of the Great Camps in the Adirondacks. Small-paned windows are another signature of this beloved style.*

OPPOSITE: *Using the gifts of nature for home accents is one of the joys of finishing a log cabin. Patterned bark and peeled twigs highlight the four panels of this door. Above, an arched window is divided by twigs, and the door handle is fashioned from a slice of shed antler. Even the door's sidelights get the natural treatment of inlaid bark.*

BELOW: *Tile is a natural for log homes. When Mother Nature gave us logs for walls, she also gave us clay for firing. Here, handmade tiles echo the hues and scenes of the forest. Granite pink, forest green, lake blue, and the mottled shades of wood are all represented, as are wild things like beavers and flowers.*

OPPOSITE: *An elegant spiral staircase becomes sculpture in this lakeside home. Dark hewn ceiling beams accent the honey tones of the walls and ceiling paneling. The wall behind the staircase gently follows the spiral's sinuous curves.*

ABOVE: *An artisanal appreciation for wood's strength and beauty can lead to fantastic details for log homes. A stout log post anchors this spiral staircase, entwined with split-log treads braced by peeled branches. A more refined wood railing and stone backdrop play supporting roles to the stairs' lead performance.*

LEFT: *The classic A-frame construction of this log home creates the perfect space for a cozy sleeping loft under the eaves. The logs used for the supports have been allowed to keep their natural shape and texture, which contrasts nicely with the smooth, flat timbers of the ceiling.*

OPPOSITE: *A wooden vanity cabinet formal enough for the living room brings elegance to a log home bath. Other thoughtful touches continue the gracious feel: tumbled tile flooring, a richly paned window, and a wood-framed mirror lit by a pair of brass sconces.*

RIGHT: *The rustic feel of logs and the sleek lines of contemporary style mingle in this master bath. Smooth white countertops and European-style cabinets fit well against the slightly rounded logs of the walls. A luxurious tub adds to the comfortable, soothing feeling that all log homes should impart.*

CHAPTER TWO

THE HEART OF THE HOME

Picture a log cabin tucked away in the northern woods. The night is frosty and dark. Powdery snowflakes are falling. Inside, lanterns glow and cast pools of yellow light out onto the snow from the cabin's small windows. Wisps of smoke rise from the cabin's stone chimney. First used for light, heat, and cooking, fireplaces were at the very core of early log cabins. Even today, a crackling fire lures us into a log cabin and sets the tone for the home's warmth and style.

Massive, open fireplaces faced with fieldstone or river rock strike a familiar note. Their looks are classic cabin style. A split-log mantel set above the open firebox helps heat radiate into the room and provides a shelf for displaying the wildflowers of summer, an antique clock, a prized mounted fish, or framed photos. Stones, rocks, or slate gathered from a neighboring forest or streambed add cool texture as they face the chimney or line up along the hearth.

But beyond the familiar stone fireplace are other hearth styles. A cast-iron, wood-burning stove recalls a hunting cabin as it spreads its warmth. Masonry heaters or *kachelovens* (Scandinavian traditional tiled heaters) warm a cabin with gentle, permeating heat while offering old-world charm. Choosing a *kiva* (a Pueblo Indian beehive-shaped adobe fireplace) invites the look of the desert Southwest into your cabin. The kiva's textured stucco glows with firelight and plays well against the smooth surface of logs. The fluid form of stucco can be used to create benches near the fire for a cozy place to curl up.

Other materials join stucco and stone around the hearth. Bricks lend subtle color and nubby texture. Delft tiles coolly recall bygone days. And soapstone, with its veining and range of colors, is both handsome and efficient in its ability to absorb heat and then release it slowly.

Hearth accessories call for personal expression. A wrought-iron tool set topped with pinecone finials echoes the forest just outside. A canvas wood tote is at home in a lakeside cottage. Rustic firewood holders fashioned from twigs uphold the Adirondack tradition. Iron fireplace screens can depict Old West wildlife scenes or a dancing Kokopelli as they guard the hearth from stray sparks. A simple basket of pinecone firestarters is a camp classic.

OPPOSITE: *Perhaps one of the sweetest joys of living in a log cabin is spending time gazing upon the flames of a hearth. A comfortable, paisley-covered chair lounges before an open rock-faced firebox. Hand-forged, oversized andirons frame the blaze. Above, a length of weathered timber serves as a simple mantel for displaying a solitary print.*

Fireplaces aren't limited to living and keeping rooms—you'll find them in other cabin rooms, too. In the kitchen, the bedroom, even on screened porches, a fireplace sparks the romance of a log cabin. Some kitchens boast wood-burning stoves outfitted with cast-iron fry pans and a blue graniteware coffeepot to revive the traditions of camp cooking.

An outdoor campfire ring or pit completes the link between hearth and home while awakening memories of camp-outs and cookouts beneath the stars. Primitive benches fashioned from split logs gather around the ring and await marshmallow roasters and storytellers.

The hearth will most likely become the centerpiece of your cabin and should reflect the style you plan to achieve. The furniture that surrounds the fireplace will be used often, by you and your guests. Make the area livable with plenty of comfortable places to sit, bright lamps to read by, and a table close at hand for holding mugs of hot chocolate and a few good books.

OPPOSITE: *A cozy, rough-stone hearth is the focal point of this casual lodge-style room. Log beams are skip-peeled of their bark for an even more rustic finish. The raised hearth is of polished stone that reflects the light of the fire. Above, a squared timber rests on two log ends to form a mantel.*

RIGHT: *Towering bookcases frame a stone fireplace with an arched firebox. A rough-hewn mantel is the display ledge for a stark photo. A copper bucket stores kindling by the fire. Leather sofas drawn close create the perfect spot for settling in with a good book.*

LEFT: *If your home has open, soaring spaces, flaunt them with open beams and a fireplace that reaches up to the ceiling. Back down in the seating area, comfy leather chairs are pulled up to an open stone fireplace, complete with raised hearth and a silvery gray wood mantel.*

OPPOSITE:

This chimney is a masterwork of twig mosaic. Twigs and bark, painstakingly applied in patterns, provide a rugged contrast to the smooth, sunshine yellow of the tiles that surround the firebox. Delft plates continue the ceramic theme, and a pair of antler sconces flanking the fireplace are another reminder of the forest outside.

OPPOSITE: *The hearth played a central role in the pioneer cabin, and today it again demands attention for its soaring form faced with river rock. The fireplace is at the home's core, defining the living room and punctuating the loft.*

RIGHT, TOP: *Twig diamonds shine above a small fireplace that tells a rustic story. The twigwork panel above the mantel is accented with papery white birch bark. Rough-and-tumble rocks form an arch over the firebox. To complete the mood, a single carved loon floats placidly along the mantel.*

RIGHT, BOTTOM: *A freestanding wood-burning stove puts the hearth at the true center of this home—in the kitchen. The stove's cheery red enamel is set off by a rust and gray slate surround and repeated in the kitchen's bright red countertops. Pinecones in a basket are ready to be popped into the fire.*

RIGHT: *Topped with a copper hood and faced with brick, this kitchen hearth recalls Old World traditions. A handy wood box is built in, while the two-sided firebox is set at eye level, allowing all in the kitchen to enjoy the comforting blaze. A stovepipe replaces the more traditional full chimney.*

BELOW: *If candlelight sets the tone for romantic meals, think how much gracious dining would be enhanced by the flicker of firelight. In ths spacious dining room, a low fireplace is topped with a refined mantel. Above it hangs a mirror that reflects the home's massive log beams.*

ABOVE: *Even outdoor rooms can be warmed by a crackling fire. The screened sunroom of this mountain summer home allows guests to linger in the well-pillowed wicker chairs and enjoy the fire long after the sun has set.*

BELOW: *A kiva sculpted from stucco accents this rustic yet decadent bathroom. Stone floors, wood beams, and a trio of deep-set windows add their share of drama to the room. A bench lit by candlelight makes a perch for enjoying the fire after a soothing bath.*

ABOVE: *The soft curves of a kiva warm and soften the corner of a loft bedroom. A handy stash of firewood allows this home's owner to stoke the fire without leaving the warmth of the bedroom. Built-in shelves make ideal display nooks for an art collection.*

CHAPTER THREE

BRINGING NATURE INSIDE

Just as Mother Nature provided logs for cabins, she also gave us the resources to furnish these homes. Wood to be sawn, twigs to be bent, and reeds to be woven all become the raw materials of log cabin furniture.

The rustic style comes to mind first when thinking of log cabin furnishings. Rustic furniture carries the integrity of natural elements crafted by hand. Made all over the world, this style was perhaps celebrated most distinctively in the sprawling compounds of the Adirondack Great Camps. There, employees of the camps spent their winters fashioning furniture for the lodges, cabins, and dining halls. They gathered twigs and logs to craft furnishings that echoed the classic styles of the Victorian era. Even when the shapes of the pieces were familiar to the Camps' high-society owners, the textures and finishes were new, adapted from the materials at hand.

Every curve and idiosyncrasy of nature was revered and kept intact by rustic craftspeople. A curved branch became an armrest or the arch of a headboard. Colored bark was used to create mosaics or to contrast with dark twigs. Twigs were split and applied in mosaic patterns to tabletops, clocks, armoires, and chests. Wood burls were collected and worked into the skeletons of furnishings. Willow branches and roots were bent into fanciful chairs and benches. Flat rocks were used to top tables. Hickory, a strong and straight wood, was used for chairs. Rustic furniture inspires a sense of wonder and appreciation of its maker's ingenuity.

Of course, not all log cabin dwellers had a staff to create furniture for them. Settlers and pioneers forever influenced log cabin style with the items they built out of necessity. Their furnishings were also made by hand, but were more practical than fanciful.

Other cabin furniture was created in the styles of Colonial and Early American pieces. Painted pine cupboards and trunks reveal their Old World roots. Some pieces were crude and primitive; others, such as Windsor chairs and turned head- and footboards, were more graciously crafted according to European traditions. The Pennsylvania

OPPOSITE: *A classic log cabin shows its roots through its bent-willow armchair and rocker. The willow branches are quite pliable when green, but after drying they become sturdy and enduring. A twig table fashioned from looped branches and topped with split twigs stands between the chairs, ready to hold a book or a glass of iced tea.*

Dutch revered the grain of hardwood furniture and painted or stained it with decorations that echoed traditional symbols of love, prosperity, and hospitality.

Another great influence on log cabin style is the look that grew out of the great migration west. In the United States, pioneers dragging their possessions in covered wagons over the treacherous terrain of the prairies and mountains were forced to cast off the furniture they brought with them. Once settled in their new territory, they need new furnishings. Log tables, chairs, and case pieces were easily crafted from peeled branches and the tall, straight pine trees that grew in abundance out west.

From this natural resource arose another fanciful, rustic tradition that has been woven into the tapestry of Western style. Twisted branches were sculpted into interesting furnishings. Antlers, shed each year by mule deer and moose, were used throughout log homes in pieces ranging from chairs to candleholders to chandeliers. Whatever nature left behind was quickly brought into the house and used.

Years passed on the frontier and the furnishings faithfully fulfilled their purposes, and then the century turned and the well-to-do tired of their retreats in the Adirondacks. They, too, began to look to the west for adventure, and they found it at the dude ranches. The popularity of the dude ranch gave rise to yet another look—Cowboy High Style. The birth of this style can be traced to furniture maker Thomas Molesworth, who was commissioned to furnish many dude ranches and hotels in the West. Wealthy easterners saw his work and requested pieces for their own homes. He combined the rustic look with the enduring images of the romantic Old West—cowboys, cowgirls, and American Indians. He created everything that a working guest ranch would need: beds, dressers, living room suites, dining tables and chairs, and writing desks on which guests could pen postcards back home. Today, reproductions of Molesworth's easily recognizable pieces furnish many log homes.

Back east, Gustav Stickley and others, inspired by the Arts and Crafts movement in England, were building clean-lined furniture that gloried in the grain of wood. Today, reproductions of these simple, expertly crafted pieces upholstered in leather or canvas fit easily into log cabins, because they share the same heritage of craftsmanship.

All the world over, cabins have been home to summer vacationers. The summer cottage tradition added yet another furnishing flavor. Cast-offs from home made their way to the cottage. Straight-backed chairs gathered around tables to create a place for solving jigsaw puzzles and playing games of Monopoly. Bunk beds topped with camp blankets made resting spots for young fishers and tuckered-out campers. Folding canvas chairs were toted to the shore. Every cottage had its wicker chair, rocker, or chaise longue. Creaky porch rockers and the softest of all cabin furniture—the hammock—are essential equipment for cottage life.

When outfitting your log cabin, remember that while many styles of furnishings can make themselves at home with logs, the overriding preference is for pieces that reveal a handmade quality. And, whatever kinds of furnishings you choose for your cabin, look for natural materials and pieces with the comfort of an overstuffed armchair.

OPPOSITE: *Perhaps no single piece of furniture defines log cabin style like the porch rocker. In shades of deep green, this pair of ladderback rocking chairs with comfortable armrests awaits summer afternoons filled with tall drinks and tall tales told beneath the shade of the log-beamed porch roof.*

ABOVE: *With primitive country furniture, form follows function and function replaces ornament. A milk-painted cupboard with a hutch is pared down to its basic essentials: shelves hidden by doors that swing from crude hinges and open with simple knobs. Still, this piece and the worn yellow straight chair beside it add homey charm to a hallway where logs contrast with plaster walls.*

RIGHT: *Today's country look is cleaner and less cluttered. A simple straight chair with a woven-rush seat stands sentry by a wooden door. The door sprouts a hand-painted garden of sunflowers, which is accented with a band of friendly blackbirds and faux wood graining.*

ABOVE: *Furniture in various styles can live together happily in a log home. A Western-inspired club chair cozies up to a rustic twig table along with a classic wing chair. Lighthearted fish upholstery adds a hint of humor to this great room.*

BELOW: *Punched-tin panels were used in pie safes to keep flies away from freshly baked goods. Here, punched tin comes out of the kitchen and dramatically fills the corner of a whitewashed log living room. The cupboard's linen hue is repeated in the soothing plaid sofa upholstery and the delicate china plate perched above.*

OPPOSITE: *Early settlers in the New World influenced the direction of American furniture. Old World traditions, evident in these chairs and the side table, include turned legs and heavy, dark wood. A photograph framed in vibrant red lightens the setting.*

RIGHT: *The silvery gray and warm sandy tones of ancient rock and weathered wood should make this room feel as rugged as the great outdoors. Instead, the well-worn leather chairs and soft Oriental rug create a haven of comfort.*

OPPOSITE: *A log passageway ends at a crude cupboard and hutch. The simple diamond pattern on the cupboard doors, the unfinished boards of the shelves, and the plain plank backing give this piece the homespun, honest charm that helps it fill its place of honor.*

ABOVE: *Ornately carved logs, such as those in this Scandinavian-style home, call for furnishings with similar sensibilities. The doors of an intricate armoire are flung open to reveal a collection of books and figurines. Muted shades of paint set off the armoire's details. Curved doors echo the piece's undulating lines.*

RIGHT: *A simple iron-strapped table, perhaps once used as a butcher's block, is now the highlight of a well-appointed log home kitchen. The table's chunky lines stand up to the massive logs in the walls and ceiling beams. The cabinetry is made of wood finished to a furniture grade.*

BELOW: *Mission-style furniture has a natural affinity for log homes, since both are centered on the love of nature and the grained beauty of wood. Heavy round logs make a wonderful foil for the squared-off lines of a Stickley dining room suite, which is anchored by a Morris-inspired rug. A simple yet elegant Arts and Crafts–style hanging lamp with a frosted glass shade casts warm, golden light on the scene.*

OPPOSITE: *Following the lead of two rustic, plaid-covered hickory chairs, a group of Old World turned side chairs gather around a thick wooden tabletop, which rests on a base made of two stout log sections. Tall, wrought-iron candleholders complete the almost medieval feel of this dining room.*

BELOW: *An exposed-beam dining area reaches back to its Early American ancestry with a turned-leg trestle table and gate-leg side table. High-back Colonial chairs circle the table. The dining area, though formal, opens in today's casual way to the kitchen, outfitted in rich cherry cabinetry.*

LEFT: *Although early pioneers would be shocked, today's log homes can go well beyond country, lodge, or rustic looks. The aesthetic of the Far East finds its way into the contemporary lines of this home. The panels of an intricate screen, the delicate nightstand, and the porcelain bedside lamps bring a touch of the Orient to log cabin style.*

BELOW: *Heavy, dark European antiques outfit this masculine bedroom. A medley of textiles furthers the Old World ambience, from the intricate carpets to the needlepoint bed pillows and the luxurious crazy quilt folded at the end of the bed. The muted colors and swirl of patterns hold their own against the log walls, which are accented with bands of chinking.*

LEFT: *A cozy bedroom stays true to its antique country-style architecture with a white iron bed, a classic wing chair, and a wooden writing desk. Limestone chinking adds chunky texture to the log walls. A woven coverlet in primary hues of red, yellow, and blue drapes over the bed.*

BELOW: *A classic club chair in weathered leather rests in a corner of a log bedroom. The room's masculine feel is underlined by the simple shape of the bedside lamp, the deep color of the logs, the rich tones of the artwork, and the simple, uncluttered lines of the chair.*

OPPOSITE: *Open, vaulted great rooms can accommodate many furniture groupings. A refined desk is flanked by wicker armchairs, set with their backs to the main seating area, which is clustered around the fire. At the windows, more wicker chairs are poised to soak in the view.*

CHAPTER FOUR

TEXTILES AND TEXTURES

Morning sunlight filters through the bedroom's soft muslin curtains. You leave the warm patchwork quilt behind and step out onto a woolly rug. Reaching for your sweatshirt, you plan this morning's walk to the ripening blackberry patch down the road.

At its most basic, log cabin style is about comfort. Textiles make the cabin into a cozy place where you can put your feet up and not worry about sitting on the sofa in your hiking gear. So whatever textiles you bring into a log cabin have to be durable. The main distinction of all good log cabin fabrics is rugged good looks. Fabrics with texture are all-important. Wood has a soft glow that is best matched by a fabric with a landscape of its own. Picture the hand-woven coverlet of a Colonial bed, the alternating shine and nap of a Victorian crazy quilt, or the creased leather of a Western armchair drawn close to the fire.

At the cottage, cool nights usher in the tradition of wool camp blankets. A classic Hudson's Bay Company point blanket warms chilly nights and adds graphic punch with its signature bold stripes set against a creamy background. Plaid blankets by Pendleton and other woolen mills also bring color and traditional good looks. Draped over log bunk beds, they take the place of a more formal bedspread. And small throws from Pendleton allow you to bring the warmth of wool and rich color to any chair in the living room, or even out to the campfire.

Some textiles reveal a sense of place. Native American blankets, with their graphic designs and rich, earthy colors, look at home in Western and Southwestern decors. They adapt easily for use on the floor, as wall hangings, or slung over a loft railing to be admired from below. A collection of blankets looks striking stacked in an armoire.

Quilts easily settle into the setting, especially the patchwork design known as Log Cabin because, like rustic furniture, they reveal the skilled handwork of the creator. These family heirlooms shouldn't be relegated to the bedroom only. With their bold designs and colors, quilts make fascinating wall hangings throughout the house. Quilt squares can cover throw pillows on the porch, and quilted throws make a porch swing or hammock the perfect spot for an afternoon nap.

For hardworking cabin furniture, one casual wardrobe essential—denim—makes great upholstery. In shades of blue or as duck or twill

OPPOSITE: *This comfortable bedroom is made even cozier with a variety of brightly hued textiles. Striped, printed, and patchwork throw pillows add softness, and serapes lend a touch of Southwestern style.*

dyed in other colors, this casual fabric holds its own in the rough-and-tumble of cabin life. As classic as a bomber jacket, aged leather is another cabin upholstery natural. Masculine and rugged, leather has found its way onto at least one chair in every Western-style home.

At the windows, curtains and drapes should be simple. Plain muslin, calico, and striped ticking follows an Early American theme. A bold red-and-black buffalo plaid can create the backdrop for Western style, and a whimsical wildlife pattern suits the summer cottage. No fussiness is allowed in cabin window treatments. For a different look, wooden plantation shutters or blinds make a crisp and functional alternative to fabric curtains.

Think creatively about hanging fabric at your windows. A long birch branch will hold lengthy sheers, while a stretch of twine held taut by brass nails will suspend simple café curtains in the kitchen. A forked branch, peeled of its bark, can hold back a simple drape.

Many different fabric colors and patterns fit into cabin style. Beyond plaids, a host of wildlife and botanical prints and vintage flannels displaying dudes and cowpokes crop up in cabins. Simple florals and flame-stitched upholstery convey Colonial style. Accent your vintage kitchenware collection with cheerful cotton tablecloths from the 1940s, bordered with bright flowers, red and white stripes, or fruit. On the porch, awning stripes and faded floral chintz throw pillows are perfect for carefree days.

For color inspiration, simply step outside. Green trees, bright flowers, and the hues of water and stones can all translate into successful color schemes for your log home and its fabrics.

On the floor, hooked and braided rugs underline your home's look with muted colors and handmade quality. Kilims, dhurries, and other flat-woven area rugs are also welcome for their informality and graphic punch. A cozy rug by the hearth and a thick mat by the door complete the home's foundation of style.

Texture can appear in other places as well. Skip-peeled logs show patches of bark, giving a rustic touch to walls. The rough complexion of plaster walls contrasts with smooth wood, and painted accents add color to create a comfortable, welcoming log home.

OPPOSITE: *In a comfy corner, surrounded by vintage kitsch, a bent willow settee and chair mark the spot for an afternoon snack. Throw pillows in cotton floral and fruit prints charm with a sense of yesteryear's romance. On the seat cushions, navy and red ticking stripes set the tone. An Oriental rug in muted hues offers subdued texture.*

LEFT: *The warm tones of logs embrace a mix-and-match style. On the floor, a flat-woven kilim warms the terra-cotta tiles. On the bar stools, chimayo weavings add a dash of color. And on the dining chairs, with their Old World air, a golden brocade echoes the yellow glow of the logs.*

OPPOSITE: *In a room seemingly filled with wood tones, subtle patterns and colors emerge. On the floor, a geometric rug offers a pattern in shades of navy and taupe. Logs skip-peeled of their bark bring a mottled texture to the walls. Simple cloth napkins and woven placemats dress the table in informal style.*

ABOVE: *Windows left bare and a floor unadorned with carpet complement the bold texture of the skip-peeled log walls in this dining area. Other subtle textures—the smooth finish of the countertops and the softness of cotton placemats—also add interest.*

RIGHT: *Layers of bedding translate to luxury in the bedroom. A matelassé bedspread is topped with coordinating pillow shams. A plush throw stretches across the end of the bed, for when the night turns frosty. A pair of pillows upholstered in rich brocade top off the bed. Above, a square of handmade lace is pretty enough to frame.*

BELOW: *Fabrics aren't the only way to bring pattern and color into your home. Stenciled flowers twine around the window trim and provide a perch for a painted bird. Stained glass in the Tiffany-style lamp and decorative window filter light into rich colors.*

OPPOSITE: *Romancing a loft bedroom is simply a matter of adding layers of florals. An Oriental rug sets the tone, then layers of scalloped and ruffled bedding in small and large floral prints transform the bed into an oasis of comfort heightened by stacks of pillows.*

LEFT: *You can count on color to pull together disparate elements. A Native American blanket rug and plaid bedspread work together because they share the same hues of red and blue. Throw pillows covered in snippets of wool Navajo blankets add another shot of color. Narrow blinds that hide away keep the windows free of clutter.*

OPPOSITE: *The bunk room is a cabin favorite for young campers. Here, little cowpokes can bed down beneath plaid flannel comforters in branchy beds. Pillows in a homespun red check pattern cradle sleepy heads, and a fluffy Hudson's Bay Company blanket adds another layer of warmth and style. The simple woven area rugs repeat the bedding's plaid.*

ABOVE: *Patchwork quilts steal the show in a cozy loft bedroom. On the double bed, a striking quilt in navy and beige is worked in a bold geometric pattern. The pretty fan quilt on the smaller bed offers gentler hues on a white background. Wooden toys await an overnight visit from a young guest.*

ABOVE: *The graphic reds, blacks, and taupes of Navajo blankets appear throughout this rustic log bedroom. From the assortment of bed pillows to the throw rug, the graphic weavings add flair to the room's neutral tones. The red of the rug is echoed in a plush throw on the bed.*

BELOW: *A Double Wedding Ring quilt graces the bed in a dormered bedroom. Lace panels caught back at the sides of the windows add another romantic touch. The bed's quilt is echoed in a pair of quilted wallhangings displayed at the far end of the room.*

CHAPTER FIVE

GOODS AND GEAR

The windowsills are deep, the logs are glowing and warm, the furnishings are comfortable and cozy—still the picture is not complete without accessories. The log cabin is a unique home. Search for the out-of-the-ordinary to add the finishing touches. Make the cabin tell the story of you and your family—the people who hold it dear. Tell of your love for the outdoors and its wildlife, your fascination with antique weather vanes, your appreciation for classic early Americana. The lighting, artwork, and decorative accents you bring home will complete your own log cabin style.

Lighting may be the most important and functional accessory. A light fixture can firmly state your style, whether it's an antler chandelier hanging above your ranch house table, a kerosene lantern in a cottage sunroom, or a punched-tin sconce lighting the way to your Colonial home's front door. With research, creativity, and inspiration, you're sure to find fixtures to shed light on your unique style. Top off sconces and table and floor lamps with shades made of birch bark, translucent rawhide, frosted colored glass, or handmade paper.

Supplement your modern lighting with the soft glow of candlelight in your log home. Hand-dipped candles in wrought-iron holders cast warm circles of light on a tabletop or mantel. Outside, flickering candles ensconced in hurricane chimneys or a collection of vintage oil lamps will evoke your porch's pioneer ancestry.

Artwork can reflect the geographical region you've chosen for your log cabin, displaying your love of handicraft or your appreciation for fine or folk art. Logs make a wonderful backdrop for enjoying paintings, sketches, and framed photos. And the large, open spaces created by vaulted ceilings cry out for three-dimensional sculptures or wood carvings. Some carvings can be integrated directly into the posts and beams of your home by a talented woodworker.

Use your cabin to display a favorite collection, whether it's a wall full of green-handled kitchen utensils from the 1930s, a family of carved German bears, redware pottery in a corner cupboard, or a rack of weathered canoe paddles. In your cabin, as in any home, a collection will pack more punch if the items are grouped together artfully on a tabletop or wall or in a case. For a collection that fits right into log cabin life, gather up the paraphernalia of early log home dwellers— cowboys, loggers, fishers, and summer campers.

OPPOSITE: *A beautiful wooden cupboard makes a perfect display shelf for a collection of vintage handmade pottery. Antique snowshoes, earthenware jugs, and an antler reading lamp strengthen the rustic mood.*

Within your handmade home, you will more fully appreciate accessories that have been made by hand. Whether the pieces are the work of your own hands or the hands of others, they will bring spirit to your home. From hand-woven baskets to antique samplers to carved decoys, log home accessories should stay true to the pioneer heritage of making things for oneself. The tools those pioneers used make great log home collectibles, too.

With walls, floors, and even furniture made of wood, you may look to accessories to add spots of much-needed color. Pieces with subdued shine—a pewter pitcher, copper kettle, or verdigris candelabra—can also bring needed relief from the warm tones of wood. Watch for colorful items to spice up your home. Soon you'll have good reason to wheel that tag-sale red wagon home to your porch or to bring that sapphire blue bottle to your kitchen windowsill.

And for a quick splash of color, nothing tops Mother Nature's own finest accessory: flowers. Gather a bouquet of just-picked blooms in a simple white ironstone pitcher, or plant a whole field full of wildflowers outside your back door.

RIGHT: *A quartet of hanging lamps lights a hallway in a rustic, chinking-lined log home. The lamps are made of translucent rawhide stretched over iron bands. The glow is warm, yet crisp. Their light reflects off the creamy plaster of the raised ceiling.*

OPPOSITE: *Whimsy is mixed with rustic style in this vintage log home. A chandelier festooned with antlers lights the room with the soft glow of light filtered through parchment shades. A spiral stair with balusters made of spindly, unpeeled branches wraps around a smooth wood post. The twig motif is repeated in the rustic sideboard.*

OPPOSITE: *Even in a log mansion, snowshoes crossed between log pillars can fuel memories of the humble beginnings of log cabins. On the pillars, groups of copper pans hanging from iron racks add a soft shine that echoes the glow of the copper hood above the restaurant-grade oven.*

ABOVE: *Scandinavian treasures fill this simple log cabin. A woven tapestry and traditional runner grace the walls, while an ornately carved cupboard and cradle hold the owner's collection of books.*

ABOVE: *In a confident grouping, even commonplace objects take on a certain artistry. Painted wooden buckets displayed on a low cupboard glory in their handmade, working-class beauty. The pegboard above holds kitchen utensils and dried flowers that set off the golden color of the buckets. Behind is the burnished backdrop of hewn logs.*

RIGHT: *A fanciful collection commands a creative arrangement. A former china shelf is pressed into service as a display case for a tackle box full of vintage fishing lures, reels, and flies. An antique minnow bucket perches atop the case, and fishing poles adorn the wall beside it.*

LEFT: A primitive cupboard displays a collection of wooden and ceramic bowls. The bowls' subtle hues stand out against the russet patina of the cupboard's aged wood. Alongside, a gathering of vintage tins, hand-dipped candles, and cast-iron cookware replays the antique kitchen theme. Logs lined with chinking create a warm backdrop.

LEFT: *Handmade treasures—baskets, a stitched sampler, and a plaited grapevine wreath—gather around a low bench in a country-style room. A rocking chair speaks of warmth and ease. The cotton rug lightens the floor, underlining the cozy feel.*

OPPOSITE: *Simplicity is at the heart of this charming room. Vintage textiles and a hand-painted side table, chair, and hanging cabinet are set atop blue woven rag runners. A china pitcher and washbowl show how lovely functional pieces can be when allowed the limelight. Age-old logs were hewn for the home's walls.*

OPPOSITE: *In a contemporary bath, a black countertop, refined wooden cabinet, and metal sink set a sleek tone. Above the vanity, a mirror framed in birch bark is reminiscent of Adirondack style. Planes of translucent glass balance between peeled twigs, creating wall sconces with an Asian influence. To the right, a singular log post adds a final rustic touch.*

BELOW: *Almost any style is at home with logs. Victorian crystal bottles and an ornate beaded lamp add charm to a corner of this log home's bedroom. A framed photo propped on a gold-toned easel and a porcelain dish of potpourri carry the Victorian theme further. The tableau is set against understated wood shutters.*

LEFT: *Lighting can reinforce your cabin's style. A punched-tin hanging lamp sheds gentle light on a work area in the kitchen of this Colonial-style log home. Over the sink, a simple two-light fixture mimics the look of candlelight, while two real candlesticks "dance" on the window sill. On the counter sits a miniature log cabin—the perfect log home accessory.*

OPPOSITE: *In the kitchen of this vacation cottage, cabinet doors are faced with Z braces and painted a cherry red. The collection of china is easily at hand in a simple wooden plate rack. An earthenware jug and wooden bowl add to the casual scene. When the family heads home for the season, the divided-light windows in the cabin can be easily covered with pull-down, interior shutters.*

INDEX

Accessories, 20, 37, *82*, 83–84,
    84–95
  eclecticism in, *87*
  natural materials in, *31*, *34*
Adirondack style, 19–20, *30*, 37, 49
Appalachian style, 19
Artwork, 82

Bark, *41*
Barns, *24*
Baths, 20, *34–35*
  accessories, *92*
  fireplaces, *46*
Bedrooms
  fireplaces, *47*
  furnishings, *64–65*, 67
  textiles, *65*, *74–81*
Blankets, 69, *78*, *80*
Breezeways, *29*

Cabinetry, 20, *35*
Candles, 82
Chairs, *51*, 67
  dining room, *62–63*
Chinking, 19, *23*
Collections, 82, *88*, *95*
Colonial style
  accessories, *82*, *94*
  furnishings, 49
  houses, 19–20
Color schemes, 70, *72*, *76–77*, *80*, 84
Corner notches, *12*, 15
Country style
  accessories, *90*
  bedroom, 67
  primitive, *52*
  uncluttered, *53*
Cupboards, 55, *58–59*, *89*
Curtains/drapes, 70

Decorating styles, 9–10
Denim, 69–70
Dining rooms
  fireplaces, *45*
  furnishings, *61–63*
  textures, *72–73*
Dogtrot-style cabins, 20
Doors, 20
Dude ranches, 50

Early American style, 49, 70, *71*

Fabrics. *See* Textiles
Far East style, *64–65*
Fireplaces, 19, *36*, 37–38, *38–47*
Flooring, 20
Furnishings, *48*, 49–50, *51–67*
  mixing styles, *54*, *61*
  natural materials in, 49

Great Camps style. *See* Adirondack
    style
Great rooms. *See also* Fireplaces
  furnishings, *66*

Hearths. *See* Fireplaces

Kachelovens, 37
Kitchens, 20
  accessories, *86–89*, *94–95*
  fireplaces, *43–44*
  furnishings, *60*
  natural materials in, *34*
Kit log homes, *15*
Kivas, 37, *46–47*

Lean-tos, *27*
Leather, 70
Lighting, 82, *84–85*, *94*
Logs, 19–20
  skip-peeled, *72–73*

Mantels, 37
Masonry heaters, 37
Mission-style furnishings, *61*
Modern log cabins, *14–15*
Molesworth, Thomas, 50

Native American textiles, *76–77*, *80*
Natural materials
  in accessories, *31*, *34*
  in furnishings, 49
  in kitchen, *34*

Old World–style furnishings, 49, *56*, *63*

Pendleton textiles, 69
Pennsylvania Dutch, 49–50
Pioneers
  accessories of, 84
  furnishings of, 50
  log houses of, *11*, 19, *25*
Porches, *17*, 20
  enclosed, *28–29*
  fireplaces, *45*
  furnishings, *20*, *51*

Punched tin, 55

Quilts, 69, *79*, *81*

Rockers, *51*
Roofs, *8*, *24*
Rugs, 70, *76–77*
Rustic style, 49

Scandinavian style, *16*, 19–20, *59*
Southwest style, 37
Staircases, *26*, *32–33*, *85*
Stencils, *74*
Stickley, Gustav, 50
Stone, 37
Stucco, 37, *46*
Summer cottages, 50
Sunrooms, *45*

Tables, *60–63*
Textiles, *65*, *68*, 69–70, *70–81*
  bedroom, *65*, *74–81*
Textures
  wall, 70, *73*
Throws, 69
Tile, *33*, 37
Trusses, king-post, *18*
Twigwork, *17*, *41*, *43*, *85*

Upholstery, 69–70, *71*

Victorian-style accessories, *93*

Walls
  texture, 70, *73*
Western style
  furnishings, 50
  houses, *10*, *22–23*, 37
  upholstery, 70
Windows, *16*, 19–20
  accessories, *93–95*
  Adirondack style, *30*
  in modern log cabins, *15*
  shutters, *23*
  treatments, 70, *71*
Wood-burning stoves, 38, *43*